THE ROMAN

AQUA DUCKS EVERYWHERE

THE ROMANS BUILT AQUA DUCKS

EVERYWHERE

AND OTHER STUDENT PERCEPTIONS

VOLUME I

THE EASTERN HIMSFEAR

Compiled and Edited by Sidney B. Paine

Paine Publishing Company
South Carolina

Paine Publishing Company
P. O. Box ████
Greenville, SC 29608

The ideas in this book came from exact quotations but have been edited for clarity and brevity. In all cases, the author has attempted to maintain the writer's original intent.

ISBN 0-939241-39-0

Printed in the United States of America

Cover design by Ron Gunter
Illustrations by Ron and Ronnie Gunter

Acknowledgements

The author gratefully acknowledges the helpful support of Carol Thompson Harrison for layout suggestions; Ron and Ronnie Gunter for artistic suggestions and renderings; Susan Gunter for typing layout; Juanita Barnett for advice concerning publishing; and expecially for the understanding, encouragement, and advice of Elaine Brooks Paine, the author's wife.

Dedication

To the thousands of students who enriched my life
and made my teaching career so meaningful.

Introduction

Countless jokes, articles, and books have been written chronicling the misstatements of generations of students. Misspellings and misunderstandings of historical and geographical data have yielded great amounts of humerous material.

I did not start out with the intention of compiling a book on student humor, but through the years, a stockpile of amusing viewpoints finally convinced me to present these efforts with hopes that the reader would enjoy them and realize that there are many interpretations of history and geography.

Table of Contents

EASTERN HIMSFEAR

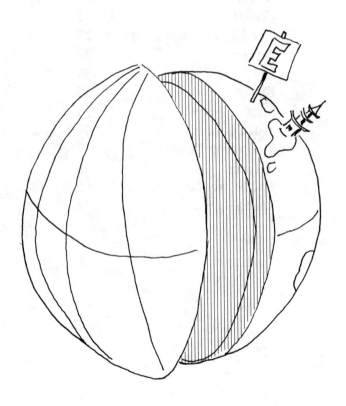

UROPE

GREASE

The beautiful temple overlooking Athens is the Pentagon.

In Athens, the only people who could be citizens were free mails.

The only citizens of Athens were men who were born and razed there.

Homer sailed on the A Jean Sea.

Three types of Greek architecture are Dork, Ironic, and Carnelian.

The Father of Medicine was the Greek physician Hiccuprotease.

Artemis was the Greek god of Haunting.

The Golden Age of Athens was led by Pairacleats.

Socrates was a poor, ugly little man until he started thinking.

Soccertees was a Greek philosopher.

Socrates asked too many questions which irked his pupil Pluto.

The first letter of the Greek alphabet is Alpo.

ROAM

Rome was founded by a wolf named Romulus.

The first Roman road was called the Appalachian Way.

The chief god of the Romans was Juniper.

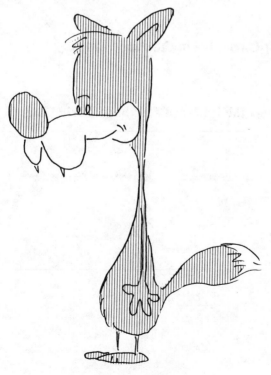

In 509 B. C., the Romans defeated the Eruptions.

The ruling class in Rome was called the Partitians.

The Romans put a lot of Muriels on their walls.

Rome fought Cartridge in the Punic Wars.

Hannabell was the leader of Carthage during the Puny Wars.

Julius Caesar said, "I came, I saw, I conked!"

Julius Seizure was stabbed in 44 B. C.

Julius Caesar said, "And you too, you brute?"

Marc Antony married Cleopatra and she then killed herself by biting an asp.

Augustus Caesar began the period known as the "Pox Romantic."

The gladiators fought in the Calcium.

At the Circus Maximus, the Romans held carrot races.

The Romans built aqua ducks everywhere.

Thousands were killed when Mount Vespucci erupted on Pompey.

Nero had little self a steam so he fiddled a lot.

Rome was sacked by the Busygoths.

FRANTZ

The capital of France is Pairs.

The chief river of southwestern France is the Roan River.

To the west of France is the Bay of Biscuit.

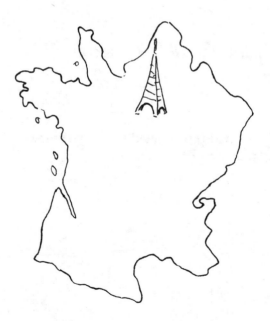

One of the leading tourist spots in Paris is the Eyefull Tower.

A favorite tourist resort in southern France is Niece.

Near France, in Manaco, is a gambling casino called Monty Carlos.

Notre Dame Cathedral is famous for its flying buttocks.

Notre Dame Cathedral is protected from evil spirits by beasts called gargles.

Joan of Art was a French heroin.

Joan of Arc managed to win a giant victory by beating off an army of 10,000 Englishmen.

Joan of Arch was at a steak burning.

Joan of Ark died because somebody sainted her.

Marie Antoinette was beheaded because she wanted people to eat some cake.

A popular French outdoor game was coquette.

A great French woman was Eleanor of Aspertaine.

THE UNITED KINGDOME

The United Kingdom is 94,226 square miles which is slightly smaller than Organ in the United States.

The major river of England is the Thymes.

London is located on Tim's River.

The Dumday Book listed people in England.

The western part of Great Britain is called Wells.

The capital of Whales is Cardigan.

North of England is Scotchland.

The largest city in Scotland is Gasglow.

The Perspireterian Church began in Scotland.

One ruler was Mary, Queen of Scouts.

Northern Ireland is sometimes called Ulcer.

The British lord was descended from two prominent families and was considered well-breaded.

King John was forced to singe the Magma Carter.

Henry VIII devoiced his wife.

Henry VIII was a member of the two door family.

The son of the lord of the castle was taught by a Tudor.

The king and his council met in a privy.

The English defeated the Invincible Ramada.

While waiting for the Armada, Sir Francis Drake spent his time boweling.

Shakespeare wrote *Rambo and Juliet.*

The inventor of gravity was Isick Neutron.

England was the birthplace of the Industrial Revelation.

Queen Victoria rained for over forty years.

During World War II, Winston Churchill was the prim minister.

The chunnel runs behind the English Channel.

The Archbishop of Canterbury is head of the Crutch of England.

The colony of New York was given by the king to his brother, the Duck of York.

British political parties were the Tarries and the Wigs.

A strange case in the United Kingdom was that of Dr. Jello and Mr. Hide.

Windsor Castle's bedrooms were filled with pantings and antiques.

JEREMY

Germany is separated from France by the Rhino River.

Most people in Germany are either Catholics or Prostates.

Martin Luther attached his ninety-five feces to a church door in Wittenburg.

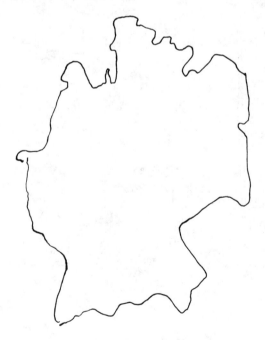

Beethoven wrote a fugue in A minus.

The leader of Germany during World War II was Adolph Hiliter.

In Germany in the 1930's and 1940's, the major political party was the Knotsy Party.

One of the world's strongest currencies is the Douche Mark of Germany.

ITLY

Italy and Greece are separated by the Iodine Sea.

Between Italy and Yugosalvia lies the Aquatic Sea.

East of Italy lies the Dramatic Sea.

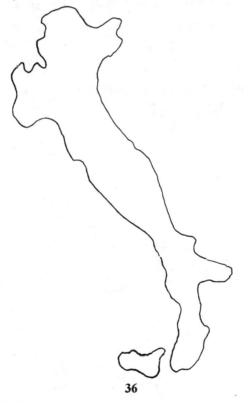

A small country located on the Italian peninsula is Sand Marinade.

South of Italy is the island of Malted.

A romantic city in northeastern Italy is Vince.

Michelangelo did the sealing on the Sixteen Chapel.

Leonardo painted the Moan Ole Lisa.

The dictator of Italy during World War II was Benito Musclelini.

Benito Mussolini was also called Ill Douche.

Italy is known for its whine making.

Italian money is called the liar.

RUSHA

North of Russia is the Barren Sea.

One of Russia's harshest Tsars was Ivan the Terrier.

Russia was led into the modern world by Peter the Grape.

The Russian pheasants were very poor and led hard lives.

Russia was led during the Revolution by John Lennon.

Russian cavalrymen were called cassocks.

The center of government in Moscow is the Gremlin.

The author of the *Communist Manifesto* was Carla Markets.

There are fifteen republics in the Soviet Onion.

The Warsaw Pact was made up of eastern European countries including the Solvent Union.

Poland and Estonia were alloys of the Soviet Union.

Latvia and Lithuania were saddlelights of the Soviet Union.

When the U2 plane was shot down over the USSR, the American pilot ejaculated.

In the middle of Moscow lies an embalmed figure of
Linen.

SPANE

Spain is part of the Eyebeerian peninsula.

Ferdinand and Isabella drove the Moores out of Spain.

Ponce de Leon helped drive the Moors out of Granola.

Christopher Cumulus sailed for Spain, but he really was an Eyetalian.

In 1492 Columbus and his semen sailed across the Atlantic to a new world.

One of the ships that Columbus commanded was the Pinto.

Columbus discovered the Diminishing Republic.

One Spanish explorer was Hernando de Soda.

Cortes was of Spanish decent.

One of Spain's greatest explorers was Vascular Balboa.

Balboa cited the Pacific Ocean in 1513.

When Balboa died, he was sentenced to death.

The Spanish colonel period lasted for over 300 years.

Pizarro's father was an infant captain.

Pizarro was an illegible child.

Pizarro took part in an expectoration of the northern coast of South America.

Pizarro concord Pure.

Francisco Pizza conquered Peru.

Magellan's parents were members of the mobility.

When his sailors muttonied, Magellan had them arrested.

Magellan was the first European to sail on the Specific Ocean.

Magellan circumscribed the world.

Magellan clammed the Pacific for Spain.

A famous writer in Spain was Sir Vantes.

A well known painter in Spain was El Gecko.

MORE UROPE

The country north of Greece is Albino.

The great church of Greece is called the Greek Orthodocks Church.

Christians is eastern Europe are called Eastern Orthodontists.

The ruler of Yugoslavia was Joseph Bronze.

The Yugoslavian leader was called Toto.

Part of the former Yugoslavia is Suburbia.

One of the countries that came out of Yugoslavia was Slowveins.

The Serbs killed a lot of Muslins in Bosnia.

Groups fighting in Bosnia were known variously as Serves, Serfs, Curbs, Slobs, and Slabs.

The capital of the Czech Republic is Prog.

A person from Poland is called a polder.

The Polish astronomer Copernicus said the plants revolted around the sun.

The poor people of Europe were called surfs.

The History of Europe was divided between the Evil and Midevil periods.

Peasants used hoursz and owks to plow.

Switzerland is bored by France, Italy, Austria, Liechtenstein, and Germany.

The capital of Switzerland is Burn.

Switzerland is dominated by the Al Paine Mountain system.

Switzerland was a neutered country during World War II.

The great Austrian musician and composer Mozart was considered a child progeny.

The mountains dividing Spain and France are called the Pairaknees Mountains.

The capital of Portugal is Lesbian.

The country between the Netherlands and France is called Belligum.

The Neitherlands used to be called Holland.

To keep the sea out, the Dutch built many dikes.
Dikes are small dames.

Dutch money is called the glider.

One of the seas of Europe is the Ball Tick.

The Kingdome of Sweden has a monarch.

Next to Sweden is Norweigh.

West of Sweden is Noway.

Sweden is located on the eastern side of the Scandinavian Penis.

The capital of Norway is Solo.

The fiord is a Norwegian car.

The capital of Ireland is Dubland.

A political group in Ireland is Shin Feign.

During World War I a popular song was "It's a Long Way to Temporary."

EURPEEING RELIGION

The largest church in Europe is the Ramon Catlick Church.

The major religion of Europe is the Roman Cattlelick Church.

The head of the Roman Catholic Church is the Poop.

The Pope leads the Roman Chaotic Church.

The Pope lives in Vacation City which is in the middle of Rome.

In 1494 the Pope divided the earth by consulting a bull named Toro de Sillas.

Many people in Europe are Roman Cathoholics.

A monarch is head of a monastery.

Clergy had to take vows of puberty, chestitty, and obesity.

Women who took religious vows were called nouns.

A female clergy was called a None.

A. D. means after deaf.

A. D. means Anne Dominated.

A. D. means anode dominoes.

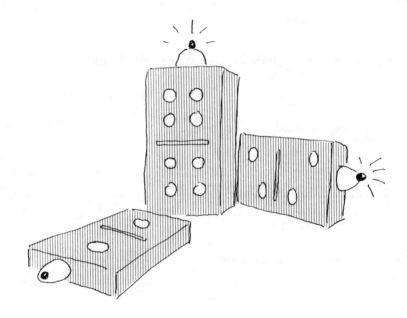

AFREECA

Egypt is bordered by Sudden and Libya.

Egypt's lifeline is the Nail River.

A huge waterway in Egypt is the Suzy Canal.

A country between Egypt and Algeria is called Labia.

The assignation of Anwar Sadat threw Egypt into turmoil.

The major pyramids are located at Geezer.

Egyptian farmers irritated their crops with water.

Ancient Egyptians wrote in hydroglyphics.

Egyptians liked music so much they buried their organs with them.

The Egyptians didn't want to dye, so they mummified their bodies.

Tut was a pariah of Egypt.

Tut became a farrow at a young age.

Tut was married to a lady named Widow.

Tut was preserved by muffication.

Tut's thumb was found by Howard Carter in 1929.

Tut's tomb is in the Volley of the Kings.

THE MITTEL EAST

The Sumerians irrigated their rivers.

The Baby Loins lived in Mesopotamia.

Persia is now called Iron.

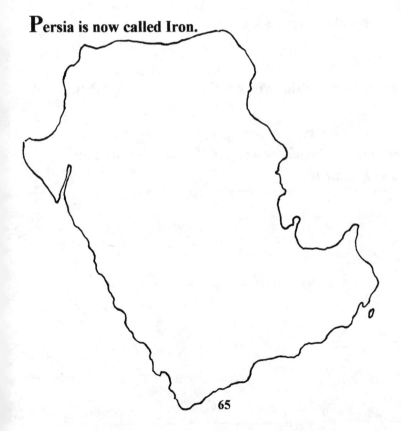

A country of the Arabian penisula is Yeoman.

The capital of Turkey is Acura.

The capital of Syria is Damask.

Cereal I was a saint who developed a new alphabet.

Between the Bosporus and the Dardanelles lies the Sea of Mammary.

The Arabs were pneumatic and moved around to find water.

Arabs lived in tints in the dessert.

Muslims worshipped in a Musk.

God gave Moses the Ten Comments.

Israel's God was named Yahoo.

The Hebrews and the Shebrews lived hard lives in Israel.

Noah and his wife Joan took in animals two-by-two into the Arc.

The ark finally came to rest on Mount Arafat.

A rock is a country in the Middle East.

Iraq is just west of the Person Gulf.

The wars in the Middle East were between the Arids and the Jaws.

In the Golf Wars, the US fought the Irakeys.

A leader in Erock is Sudden Whosane.

Iraq's dictater is Sodomy Husane.

Sadman Hosane is the leader of Iraq.

The leader of the Palestinians is Yes Sir Arrowfat.

The PLO leader is Yessir Earfat.

The Prime Minister of Israel is Knittin Yahoo.

ASHEA

Asia is in the Eastern Himsfear.

A hurricane in the Pacific Ocean is called a tycoon.

A hurricane in the Indian Ocean is called a sigh clone.

The religious leader of Tibet is the Daily Lima.

Tibet's religious leader is the Deli Lambda.

The Abdominal Snowman lives in Asia.

One Asiatic language is karate.

In the Indian Ocean are the Cormorant Islands.

The capital of India is New Deli.

The Hindus believe in rain carnation.

Southeast Asia was known as Indoor-China.

A beautiful country in Southeast Asia is Thighland.

The Khmer Rough ruled Cambodia for years.

In Singapour, an eighteen year old American boy was wiped with a bamboo cane.

Ferdinand Marcos was on a kidney diameter.

Tumor is in east Indonesia.

The United States fought in North Vitamin for many years.

The country with the most people is Chain.

For many years, China was ruled by Chairman Mouse-A-Tongue.

The Chinese broke up pro-democracy demonstrations in Tenement Square.

China's great desert is the Goobi.

A country north of China is Magnolia.

The capital of Taiwan is Type-A.

Honda is a car made by the Japaknees.

The Koran peninsula is divided between North and South.

The U. S. fought a war in Asia to preserve a country in South Career.

In 1950 the U. S. fought in North Carrion.

Ah, the wisdom of youth!

If you enjoyed *Volume I: The Eastern Himsfear (The Romans Built Aqua Ducks Everywhere!)*

then

brace yourself for *Volume II: The Western Hemispear (Thomas Paine wrote Common Scents!).*

Furthermore

Paine's Corrective Map of the World is destined to become a classic.